HOW TO
— BUY A —
LAMBORGHINI

Or

JUST RETIRE EARLY AND ENJOY LIFE

by

Dorian James

The best time to plant a tree was 20 years ago. The second-best time is now.

– Chinese Proverb.

TABLE OF CONTENT

INTRODUCTION 1
CHAPTER 1 3
  EARLY RETIREMENT 3
  HOW TO RETIRE EARLY 4
CHAPTER 2 10
  INVESTING FOR EARLY RETIREMENT 10
  REQUIREMENTS TO SATISFY BEFORE INVESTING 11
  CONSIDERATIONS TO MAKE ONCE YOU START INVESTING 11
  STEPS TO GREAT INVESTING 14
  HOW TO FUND EARLY RETIREMENT INVESTMENTS 17
  BEST INVESTMENT PLAN FOR EARLY RETIREMENT 19
CHAPTER 3 30
  POSSIBLE RISKS THAT MAY ARISE FROM EARLY RETIREMENT INVESTMENT 30
  HOW TO HANDLE INVESTMENT RISKS 32
CHAPTER 4 36
  HOW TO WORK FOR EARLY RETIREMENT 36
  POSSIBLE JOBS THAT WILL ALLOW YOU TO RETIRE EARLY 37
  HOW EARLY RETIREMENT OPENS YOUR EYES TO NEW OPPORTUNITIES 39
CHAPTER 5 42

HOW TO CREATE A WORK LIFE BALANCE THAT GUARANTEES EARLY RETIREMENT 42

ACHIEVING EARLY RETIREMENT SUCCESS THROUGH INVESTMENT 44

POSSIBLE INVESTMENT PLANS TO CONSIDER DURING EARLY RETIREMENT 45

CHAPTER 6 51

HOW TO DISCOVER POSSIBLE INVESTMENT OPPORTUNITIES AFTER EARLY RETIREMENT 51

MAKING YOUR SAVING WORK FOR YOU AFTER SERVICE 52

BEST INVESTMENT OPPORTUNITIES NO ONE IS TALKING ABOUT 54

CHAPTER 7 57

BENEFITS OF EARLY RETIREMENT 57

PROS AND CONS OF EARLY RETIREMENT 57

THE CONS OF RETIRING EARLY INCLUDE; 58

WHEN TO INVEST AFTER RETIREMENT 60

CHAPTER 8 61

HOW GOOD FINANCIAL PLANS CAN INFLUENCE YOUR INVESTMENT DECISIONS 61

KNOWING WHEN TO CONSULT AN EXPERT 63

THE DIFFERENT FINANCIAL PLANNERS 64

MISTAKE TO AVOID WHEN HIRING A FINANCIAL EXPERT 66

METHODS OF MAKING MONEY 68

CHAPTER 9 69

BUDGETING FOR YOUR EARLY RETIREMENT INVESTMENT 69

HOW TO BUILD A BUDGET 70

ON REDUCING EXPENSES 71

WAYS OF REDUCING EXPENSES 72
HOW TO FINANCE AN INVESTMENT PLAN 75
LEARNING MORE ABOUT THE BEST COMPANIES TO INVEST IN...76
HOW TO INVEST IN PUBLIC COMPANIES? 82

CHAPTER 10.. 87
THE NEED TO MAKE PLANS AHEAD OF TIME..............................87
HOW TO AVOID POOR INVESTMENT IDEAS 88
BUILDING A NEW LIFE AFTER RETIREMENT.................................91

INTRODUCTION

Most of us work. Most of us make money. But almost all of us think that investing is just for rich folks that have a deep understanding of the economy, markets and have deep enough pockets in case anything goes wrong.

That is just not true anymore.

Nowadays everyone can not just save but invest money now to make a huge impact on his life down the line. Depending on what your goals and means are we are going to explore different strategies, talk about building wealth, and all of that while being very responsible with our money and never too aggressive.

If you are looking for a get-rich-quick scheme this is not it!

The goal is to slowly but steadily raise your net worth with sound, diversified investments until you have enough to retire early and enjoy your life to the fullest with your over the years accumulated wealth.

I hope you enjoy this guide and learn from it.

Dorian James

CHAPTER 1

EARLY RETIREMENT

Earlier on, when you get paid your monthly salary, a portion of your paycheck is deducted and sent to Medicare and social security. That means a retirement plan has already been created for you whether you are aware or not. Much of it has changed today and there is an increasing need for you to be in charge of your retirement.

What do you think about retirement? Is it hours spent lazing out in the beach, watching the blue waves lap at the sand? Whatever you perceive retirement as, you no longer want to hit the snooze button and dress up to go to work.

Having an early and successful retirement is not really the point. Retirement is more like a lifestyle. It doesn't happen when you retire, it begins the very moment you decide you want to retire early.

Retirement is the act of creating goals and plans that involve your future, and carrying out those activities that draw you closer to achieving those goals. Asides being a financial plan, it is also a life plan. Just like life, retirement is a journey, and the only hero in that journey is you. Let's begin.

HOW TO RETIRE EARLY

This chapter will guide you on the steps you can take to achieve the early retirement you desire. But before you go into the how of retiring early, there are some smart things you must take note off:

Take a high route

Your target is an early retirement so you cannot afford to get involved in anything that will delay or derail you from your goal. So, when investing, plough a majority of your funds into stocks and mutual funds. The reason is they are speedy and dependable means of achieving your retirement goals. However, be cautious. Refuse to get carried away. You need to ensure your investment can deliver on it returns to you.

No shortcuts

Shortcuts are nothing but deceptive routes promising you a quicker means only to derail you from your goals. While the desire to achieve your retirement goal faster may be compelling, taking many shortcuts can backfire. It is far better to arrive at your goals, slowly, steadily and surely. Some of these shortcuts are investment with aggressive risks targeted at making you richer faster. They include forex, high risk stocks, day trading and so on. while they are not necessarily bad, they can set you back big time if you invest solely in them.

Now we are done with that, let's get on to the steps you can take for an early retirement:

1. Know why you want to retire early

Why do you want to retire early? Answering this will give you more clarity as you journey to being an early retiree. You will need to create a why list. This list holds the key reasons an early retirement matter to you. It also serves as the motivation to keep on with your plan and helps you to remain focused.

You can write on your why in a journal or a sheet of paper. To determine your why, ask yourself:

-what are my top five hobbies

-do I spend time on my hobbies?

-If I had no financial concerns, what amount of tie would I dedicate to those hobbies.

-what activities will I partake it assuming I was financial free?

Those are not set in stone. Give yourself as many whys as you can. They will help you fine-tune the lifestyle you desire.

2. Level up:

So, you want to retire early, do you have an income producing job? Or preferably a skill set that churns in money? Now, I'm not talking about minimum wage. You need to invest in yourself educationally and skill wise to earn more. In fact, to retire at all, the first thing you need is to have a source of income. To retire much earlier, your income source must be bringing in a solid amount of money that can cater for your needs and expenses without hassle.

It doesn't matter if you are the hardest worker in your workplace. If the income is low, you will be less motivated to out in your best. Instead, dedicate time to increase your value in the marketplace. Learn a high-income skill like digital marketing, copywriting, high ticket closing, become a consultant, or switch careers to a field with higher demand. You are paid what you are worth, invest in yourself.

3. Know the retirement lifestyle you want

You need to determine your ideal retirement lifestyle before you begin any retirement plan. Is your current lifestyle the same as your desired lifestyle? Will you take vacations, dine in 5-star hotels, go o shopping sprees or live modestly? Knowing what you want will inform you on the price you have to pay to get them.

4. Pay all your debts

Debt is the enemy of your progress. It is the bloodsucking quicksand that will stop you from reaching your retirement dreams. As long as debt is present, you will neither be free psychologically nor financially. Clear debts fast.

5. No more delays, get saving

Time is an asset. The earlier you begin saving, the earlier the power of compound interest works for you. Saving early will give an edge and allow you to retire much earlier than you wish.

6. Keep your expenses low

Financial demands will also pop up. You need to determine which one is worth putting your money into or seeking another alternative for. Money, as easy as it is to make, is easier to lose. Good money management will then keep you grounded. One of such is having low expenses. Just like debts, expenses are money sucking. They leave your pockets into the hands of another. While some expenses are unavoidable such as food, transportation, ensure that they are not pocket draining. Look out for high quality and cheaper alternatives if there's an expense you cannot afford to miss out on. Also, evaluate the nature of that expense if it's worth spending on or not.

7. Invest in retirement plans

Retirement plans like the 401k allow you to have a secured retirement. With a retire plan, you invest for your future security and also gain massive tax benefits. The benefits you gain in a business are many. As an employer, your contributions are made to be tax deductible. Also, your assets grow without being tax and you can explore different plan options. Investing in a retirement plan increases your tax credits and helps you reduce costs.

As an employee, if you invest in a retirement plan, your contributions reduce your taxed income. Those contributions and the gains you make on every investment will not be taxed until you withdraw, and you can easily make contributions by letting your employer deduct them. Your interest accumulates with time, and by the time you are ready to retire, you would have a healthy nest egg.

A retirement plan also allows you to move your assets whenever you change jobs and sometimes, your credit as a saver will be available to you.

8. Know your retirement needs

You need to determine how much you need to live on an annual basis. Expenses will not vanish overnight, in fact, they are more likely to increase as the years progress due to the inflation. Although, if you now have grown up kids in their own homes, you can expect no expenses from that front.

To calculate your retirement income, take your current income and multiply it with 80-90 percent.

SAVING FOR EARLY RETIREMENT

Saving for retirement is an important yet underrated step many Americans hardly take to build their nest egg. Statistics show that as at 2020, almost 50% of Americans had set saving of money has one of their new year resolutions. It is interesting to note that a good number of people think of saving, yet thinking without a corresponding action produces no effect.

Saving for retirement is actually easy. You can make use of the following steps to get started:

First, have a retirement goal. If you want to go on a trip, you would have already determined the destination and created a plan to get there. In the same vein, have a clear retirement goal with a set plan to fulfill it. Your retirement plan should be specific enough so you will be focused enough to get it done.

Second, invest 20% into tax friendly accounts. If you are in a full time or part time job, check out the retirement plans your employer offers. If the traditional 401(k) is available, invest the match to key into free dollars. If your company is offering a Roth 401(k), you can choose to invest the entire 20% so long the mutual funds options are worthwhile.

Third, max out your retirement account and additional investments. If you want to invest more than 20%, ensure your 401(k) and Roth IRA are completely maxed out. You can also open a taxable investment. This account allows you to add as much money as you want and withdraw whenever you please. As your money grows, your account will be taxed. You can also set aside an emergency fund, and buy some local real estate properties that will appreciate with time.

CHAPTER 2

INVESTING FOR EARLY RETIREMENT

Investing is a crucial activity you must partake in if you want a stress-free future. With the occurrence of the COVID pandemic, a supposedly strong economy can be brought to its knees. Only the unprepared were taken off guard financially. Those who managed their investments properly recorded wins as the market has major turnovers in the last six months of 2020.

Investing is essential to wealth building. It provides an additional income source, and can help you achieve your retirement goals, while increasing your financial power.

So, if you happen to have some spare cash, leaving it in a non interest account is no longer an option. Rather, investing it in a bunch of investments either conservative or risky is a far better choice.

You can invest in diverse ways. You can select investment from conservative options like CDs and money market, medium risk such as bonds or even risky like stock index funds. Choosing different investments with different returns helps you to create a diversified and safer portfolio.

REQUIREMENTS TO SATISFY BEFORE INVESTING

You cannot jump right into the investing game. There are certain qualifications you must possess before you can invest your money:

1. You are debt free. You have no loans or mortgage to pay off.
2. You have at least three to ten months' worth of expenses in your emergency funds.
3. You have an insurance policy, whether you are disabled or not.
4. You have a good life insurance.
5. You are health insured.
6. Your home has been insured

CONSIDERATIONS TO MAKE ONCE YOU START INVESTING

Before you invest, there are certain factors you need to evaluate. These factors are important because they determine the approach you will take when investing. Also, they must be in line with your retirement goals.

Sone factors to consider include:

1. Risk tolerance

This determines the level of risk you can tolerate when the value of your investments fluctuate. Your risk tolerance is also psychological and is based on your financial needs. It will determine the type of portfolio you will create.

If you are conservative or close to retirement, you are more likely to allocate a larger portion of your portfolio to low-risk investments. This is an excellent choice for those with short term and middle term goals. Also, the volatility of the market will affect investments like CDs and Fdic protected accounts to a lesser degree.

If you are more aggressive or still have more time to gather your retirement funds, you may choose riskier assets. Ensure that those assets are diversified to spread the risk and reduce the chances of the entire portfolio from crumbling.

9. Time range

Time range here refers to when you need your money. Will it be the following day or in a decade? Are you saving for your retirement or to purchase a property? The time you will need your money back determines the investments you invest in.

If your time range is short, the money must be in your account at a specific time and not later. So, the investments you will make will be safer and more conservative. Investments such as CDs, savings accounts or sometimes bonds fall in here since they are less volatile.

If your time range is longer, you will benefit more from higher risk investments. The time range will allow your investments to outlast market fluctuations, and gain more in the long run. Investments such as stocks and stock funds fall into this category as you can keep them for a minimum of three years and more. In all, calibrate your investments in your time range so you will not end up making wrong investment decisions.

10. Your investment knowledge

What you know about investing will determine what you invest in. CDs and savings accounts for instance need little knowledge since those accounts are FDIC protected. Other investments such as stocks and bonds require a deeper knowledge of how they work.

Also, when investing in assets that demands deeper knowledge, you want to ensure you understand how they work. For example, if you are investing in stocks, you want to know more about the company, products, the industry itself, the financial state of the company and lots more.

However, there are a lot of people who have little time to accumulate knowledge for investments like this. You can still claim a portion of the market even if you are not knowledgeable. One way to do this is buying index funds. Index funds contains a bunch of stocks. If one stock underperforms, the index will not be affected much. The reason is as you buy an index fund, you are investing in dozens or hundreds of stock options.

But in all things, your level of knowledge plays a role in your investment's decisions.

11. Level of income for investment

How much are you willing to invest in? More money means that you are more likely to invest in riskier and higher interest investments.

Also, more money will mean that you invest in understanding the industry and investment you want to make because the returns and risks are far higher than a conservative option like CDs.

If that is not the case, invest in mutual funds or bank products that require little time investments. They work for those who want to increase their retirement funds.

STEPS TO GREAT INVESTING

Investing is not a one-time activity but a life time activity. The proceeds from your investments are what will help you to retire early and support the rest of your life. You don't have to spend time learning how investing works. Sure, you can read books, watch YouTube videos and attend online and offline seminars to learn more about investing. However, you can invest with the knowledge you have.

The first step to great investing is to be an aggressive saver. The reality is that you cannot invest without money, and having savings set the precedent for your investments. Saving will not make your money grow fast, but in a good savings account, it can accumulate solid earnings in the long term. Also, saving early goes a long way in helping you make those additional interests.

Being an aggressive saver is far better than being an aggressive investor. The reason is with savings, you have greater control but when it comes to investing, the market is outside your control. Also, saving little and late will compel you to invest aggressively because you want to catch up with those lost time. That is a risk a you can lose all your money and that will take more time for you to bounce back.

The second step to great investing is to defeat taxes and inflation. Both taxes and inflation are the obstacles to your financial dreams. Inflation reduces the purchasing power of a dollar each year. Taxes are the percentage you pay for earning money. Because of these two, investing too safely will not allow your investments to stay above inflation.

Inflation doesn't only affect your returns. It nips always at both the interest and the capital. And it takes even longer for the interest to make up for that damage. Aside the usual government taxes, you are also required to pay invests taxes in taxable accounts.

While tax evasion is a crime, tax avoidance is not. By avoiding taxes on your taxable investments, that means you invest in mutual funds with little turnover of stocks. That way the gains you make will not be noted as dividends. If the stocks are directly owned by you, the little returns mean that you have little capital gains. Also, holding your stocks for the long term reduces the chances of government taxing you. So, allow your investments to compound for the long term is a solid strategy.

Inflation is unavoidable. To beat inflation, you need to invest to allow your money grow faster, beat taxes and exceed inflation rate. You can aim to increase your investment returns by at least 3% per year to beat inflation. This is not possible every year though as the stock market fluctuates.

The third step is to think like an investor. How does an investor think? Long term. The market is a playground. Everyone is trying to cash in some dough. There is no perfect way to invest. The most reliable way is through experiences and that Is as diverse as the colors of a rainbow.

Also, people are different when it comes to money. Just as they are different in the areas of wants and needs, investing personalities and financial goals. So, you will need to work out your difference to find the perfect fit for you.

The fourth step is be careful of yourself. Oh yes, we can be our own worst enemies because of money. That is owing to two factors: fear and greed. Fear stops us out of the market when the market moves in an unfavorable way. It wants us to wait until the market has recovered, but by missing out, you may not know when that has happened if you are not in it. The fear of recording losses can make one forget about long-term investing especially when the market is dropping. Always keep informed that the market's always changing. It doesn't stay down for long. It is always moving on.

On the flip side, greed keeps us in the market when its booming. You may find yourself trending stocks or funds in their best days. Greed can make you forget about your investment plan so that you can gain more out of the market. Then when the market flips, it is at your expense.

HOW TO FUND EARLY RETIREMENT INVESTMENTS

When it comes to funding your retirement investments, the most important factor is starting early. When you begin on time, you allow the power of compound interest work for you. However, irrespective of the time you begin your retirement plan, there are many ways you can boost your savings for your dream retirement.

It all begins with saving

Start now to save. Save as much and as often as you are able to. By doing so, you allow compound interest to boost the earnings your assets will generate, which will be reinvested to work favorably for you.

Make contributions to your 401(k) account

Take advantage of the traditional 401(k) account your employer offers if you are eligible for it. If a Roth 401(k) is offered instead, decide if it's the right choice for you and act on it quickly.

Match your employee

Once your employer matches your 401k contributions, ensure to make contributions so that you can enjoy the benefits that come with the match. That is practically free money you can use to boost your retirement funds. Don't miss out.

Use catch up contributions

The importance of starting early cannot be overemphasized. But if you have reached 50 years or exceeded it, you can make use of catch-up contributions. Catch up contributions allow you to exceed the usual retirement savings limit., so you can put in more money to fund your retirement plan.

Savings automation

You can fund your account without much efforts by automating the process. You can automate the saving to specific retirement accounts.

Plough in the bonuses

Another way to fund your retirement is by dedicating a percentage of those extra pennies you were gifted or rewarded at work to your retirement plan. While it is tempting to spend that extra money on a splurge, rather give yourself a smaller treat and increase the level of your future income.

Invest in startups

This is another great way to fund your retirement plan. You don't necessarily have to been a business owner, rather you can choose to be an investor in a small business or established institution. Even if you choose to be a business person, one great thing is that the profits small business make is uncapped and the ROI is potentially higher compared to other investment types. Before investing, do your due diligence by researching the company.

BEST INVESTMENT PLAN FOR EARLY RETIREMENT

There are many investments plans you can take advantage of for an early and enjoyable retirement. None by itself is the best, but each is unique and provides certain benefits for potential retirees. Note that retirement plans are generally tax advantaged, either during savings or withdrawals.

Individual Retirement account (IRA)

This is an invaluable retirement plan the United States government created to support workers in saving for retirement. Participants are allowed to make contributions of at most $6000 between 20201 and 2021. If you are above 50 years, you can contribute maximum of $7000.

Ira plans are diverse and versatile. Let's explore each of them.

The Traditional IRA

This IRA is a tax friendly plan that gives you huge tax breaks while saving for your retirement. As long as you earn money and make contributions, those contributions are pre-taxed. That means, your contributions grow tax free until you retire. Once you retire and make withdrawals, your money will be taxed. If you make early withdrawals, you will be heavily penalized.

This investment plan is a popular option among those planning to retire early. It provides immense tax benefits. You can also buy a wide variety of investment, from stocks to bonds and real estate among others. The highlight of this plan is you don't pay tax until you reach the age to withdraw our money.

On the flip side, removing money form this account can cost you more in terms of taxes and penalties. You are also required to invest by yourself regardless of the asset type. So, you will need the help of a financial adviser.

Roth IRA

This is a relatively current version of the traditional IRA. It also provides immense tax benefits. Unlike the traditional IRA where your contributions remain untaxed until retirement, the Roth IRA taxes your contributions. The high side is that there is no need to pay taxes once you withdraw on retiring. Also, the Roth IRA allows you to withdraw money at any time without additional costs and penalties.

You are given full control over your investment decisions. Yet will be prudent to seek the help of an experienced financial adviser. There are also some limits on your contributions to this plan.

Spouse IRA

While this plan is for workers with disposable income, it also allows the spouses of those workers to contribute to an IRA too. The spouse IRA can either be traditional or Roth IRA. This retirement plans allows your spouse whether he or she is working or not, to partake in retirement benefits. But you also have to decide on which investment to make.

Rollover IRA

The moving of one retirement account into another a new retirement account creates the rollover IRA. When you roll the funds from one ira account to another, you can still benefit from the tax advantages of a retirement account. Rolling over your ira can be done at any institution as long as you allowed to do so. The rollover ira can either be a traditional or Roth ira and you are limited to the amount of money you can transfer to your rollover retirement account.

With this account type, you can change your retirement account from a traditional to a Roth ira. To do this, you are required to create the rollover ira, then effect the transfer of funds. Do note that some transfers can accumulate taxes, so do your diligence before making them.

The rollover account provides an easy way to change your retirement account. You can also use it to improve your finances.

Even with a rollover account, your investment decisions are made by you. Note any additional tax payments you will need to make if you are rolling over your account.

Sep Ira

This is similar to the traditional ira, but is applicable to business persons and their workers. The employer is the only eligible contributor to this account. Contributions are made into this plan for every employee instead of a trust fund. If you are self-employed, you are allowed to create your own Sep Ira.

Between 2020 and 2021, the limit for contributing o this plan is $57,000 or a 25% of every compensation. It gets more complicated for individuals who are self-employed.

This is practically a free account for employees. For the self-employed, you are allowed to make much higher contributions and that's what makes this plan more compelling than the usual ira.

Despite the free money involved, there is no guarantee of the amount of income the employees will get from this plan. The account holders are required to make decision son on investments. If you try to get the money out before the eligible age, you will be penalized a whopping 10%.

Simple Ira

401k plans demand that employers pass through many nondiscrimination tests every year to ensure the excess amounts are not contributed by highly paid workers.

But the simple ira does not require those tests as all employees are provided equal benefits. The employee decides to contribute either 3 percent to match the employee's contribution or make 2 percent non-elective contribution whether or not the employee also contributes.

Since the simple ira is designed to offer a match, opportunities are available for workers to carry out any deferral on pre-taxed salary. This may not be different from the 401k plan.

As at 2020 and 2021, employee contributions were reduced to $13500 unlike other plans. in this plan, the employee decides on the amount to contribute and makes investment decisions on your behalf.

2. Defined Contribution Plans

Defined contribution plans were introduced in the 1980s. They have overtaken the retirement market. As at 2019, an estimated 86% of fortune 500 companies were offering defined contribution plans instead of the traditional pensions.

The 401k plan has proven to be the most commonly used plan by employers irrespective of their sizes. This plan shares the same structure with the 403b plan and the 457b plan.

As at 2021, the least an employer can contribute is $19500. For workers above 50 years, employers can contribute up to #26000.

DC plans also have Roth versions like the Roth 401k.

401k

This is a pre-taxed plan that allows you to dive for retirement. The traditional 401k allows the employee to contribute without paying taxes. As your contribution grow tax free until you retire, attempting to withdraw before the eligible age will cost you.

A Roth 401will e you contribute after you have been taxed but your gains remain untaxed when you withdraw upon retirement.

You can also automate the payment into your 401k account. The money is invested in high interest investments. Also, your employer can offer match contributions so you will be receiving free money.

However, you may not be able take loans out of your employer's fund. Additionally, your investments are limited by your employer's match so you may lack the choice of investing in your preferred program.

403b

This is the same as 401k. it is offered by charities, schools and even churches. The employers make pre-taxed matches so the contributions are not taxed. Until retirement, your funds remain untaxed. Withdrawals at retirement are taxed, and withdrawals made before retirement are penalized.

This plan is a well-known and effective way you can save for your retirement. You can automate savings into this account from your salary. The money you plough into this plan is invested in a variety of investments, from stock funds to annuities.

Your employers can also make matching contributions. Similar to the 401k, withdrawal is difficult to make in times of emergency. Even if you access the money, you will be heavily penalized and taxed. Also, you are limited in terms of making investment choices.

457b

This shares some similarities with the 401k plan. The difference is that this plan applies to only state and local government employees and some organizations that have been exempted from paying taxes.

The employees can make contributions with pre-taxed wages. This plan also allows those contributions to grow tax free until you retire. Only when the money is withdrawn does it become taxable.

This plan is highly effective for retirement because it is ta advantaged. It provides some catch-up features for much older workers compared to other pans. This plan is usually a supplement so you are not penalized for making withdrawals before the stipulated age.

While it's a great retirement plan, it doesn't allow your employer to make a match. It's more difficult to make an emergency withdrawal. This plan benefits retired workers with disabilities and needed access to their funds.

3. Solo 401k

This plan is for the business owners and their spouses. As the business owner functions as an employer and employee, deferrals of $19500 or less are allowed. If you operate a sole proprietorship for instance, this plan works far better that simple ira because you can make higher contributions to it.

Also, this pan is easy to sign up for and terminate. You can equally set up the solo 401k as Roth account.

On the flip side, once your assets go beyond $250000, you are expected to fie annual reports on Form 5500-SE.

If you will eventually increase your business and hire more workers, this plan is not ideal. This is because by hiring more workers, you are mandated by IRS to included them in your plan as long as they are eligible. The plan will also be subjected to the nondiscrimination testing.

4. GIAS

GIAS is guaranteed income annuities which individuals can purchase to create their one pensions. They are not given by their employees. You are allowed to buy an annuity immediately to get a lifetime monthly payment. If this is not convenient for you, you can choose to buy deferred income annuities. This is a more common option to get cash flow for life.

You can buy annuities after tax or from an ira with a tax deduction. However, your annuity will be taxed once you start taking withdrawals.

You need to be sure you want to retire before taking an annuity. Gias are also complex. You may find it difficult to understand the term and conditions before signing up. So, ensure to be informed about the annuity before buying.

5. Pensions

Also known as defined benefits, pensions are easy to manage since little is required of employers. Contributions are made by the employers with a monthly benefit for workers upon retirement. Sadly, only few companies actually offer retirement plans. statistics from Willid Watson show that 14 percent of Fortune 500companies got new workers with pension plans compared to 59 percent in 1998.

Since pensions demand employers to pay heavily for your retirement. these pensions are paid to depending on your tenure and the amount of salary you are paid.

Pensions help you not to you run out of money upon retirement. Since they are tied to the number of years you have served, you reap more of the benefits when your career ends.

However, if you have a change of job or get your plan terminated before you retire, you will receive lesser benefits.

6. Profit Sharing Plans

These are incentives offered by some companies to boost the productivity of their workers so that they can increase and partake of the profits the company makes as this is an incentive, you cannot make contributions to it except for your employee.

Also, your employee decides whether to make contributions on an annual basis. The federal government however stipulates that such contributions must be continuous and worthwhile.

Some profit-sharing plans allows you to select the investments you want, but they do it guarantee your financial safety. These plans are only great as supplements to your established retirement plan.

7. FERS

The federal employee's retirement plans provide a three-tier retirement offer for employees worth a basic and defined benefit plan, thrift savings plan and social security.

Once you are no longer working for the government, only two of the three are portable.

The thrift savings plan is similar to the 401k plan. The participants can select from a bunch of cheap investment options like index funds or bond fund. Government workers get 5 percent contribution matched by their employer to the test.

However, defined contribution plans present uncertainties on financial severity upon retirement.

1. Cash Value Life Insurance

Insurance vehicles are offered by some companies as benefits. Insurance are of different type, from whole life to variable universal life. All of them offer death benefits while increasing in cash value. You can use this plan to fund your retirement. After you have withdrawn your cash value, the premiums are received first and remain untaxed.

This plan deals with many risks. Growth and your interests accrued are not taxed. If not done well and the policy collapse, you will pay a heavy tax. Sometimes, the products underperformed compared to what is touted.

This plan is ideal for the rich who have maxed out their retirement plans.

You can invest in this plan if you have exceeded the limits for contributing to your 401k or ira plan.

10. Cash Balance Plan

This is a kind of pension or defined benefit. Depending on your contribution and investment credits, you are promised an account balance.

Your investment credits are promised and not determined by contribution credits. Since the benefits are promised, you may not contribute to it. If you switch jobs, you can get out the full worth of your account.

If the company becomes a cash balanced plan, workers who have worked for longer periods will lose out more. The date you choose to retire will determine the benefits you get. Worker for longer time will be to your advantage. This plan is not ideal for those who see to retire early.

Also, you have the option to select either a lump sum or a lifetime annuity.

10. NQDC

The Non-qualified Deferred Compensation plans are of two types: one similar to a 401k plan with employee match and deferrals on salary, and the second which is funded only by the employer.

This plan is exclusive available to top executives in C-suite. Most of the time, for the second NQDC plan, it is not truly funded by the employer. The employer merely makes a promise, and may be put some funds.

This plan allows you to save money while deferring on taxes. Your employer cannot not take deduction in taxes till you pay taxes upon withdrawals.

As attractive as this plan is, there is little financial security because payment is promised and at times, defaulted on. This plan works as a support to your 401k or when you have maxed out your 401k plans.

CHAPTER 3

POSSIBLE RISKS THAT MAY ARISE FROM EARLY RETIREMENT INVESTMENT

There are many risks that pose threats to your retirement investments. Knowing and understanding these risks will guide you in your investment decisions. While retirement investments are for the long term, knowledge of these risks you may experience will help you be more proactive in taking measures that will guarantee your returns.

1. Inflation

Inflation decreases your spending power with time. As a retiree, you are vulnerable considering the limited money options you have.

2. Expending your retirement funds

The heath industry has recorded massive improvement. Save for the COVID-19 pandemic, Americans are living for many more years. While this is good news, there is also the possibility of outliving your retirement funds. The longer you are alive, the lesser your assets.

3. Providing financial help to family

At a point or two, your dependents or relatives will come to you for financial support. By choosing to support them, you will record a drop in your money.

4. Interest rates

The growth of your retirement funds is dependent on the movement rate pf interest. If you want to save, borrowing from environment with little interest rates profit you in a little way because they will only pay low returns on investments with low interest rates.

5. Loss of a loved one

The loss of a spouse for instance can affect the benefits of pension. Death of a loved one can also add more financial strain to the retiree's income as there will be bills and debts to settle.

6. Market changes

This is a risk where investor loses money in an adverse market. Markets are unpredictable. They move either up and down without anyone's permission. A huge dip in the market can shrink the value of your assets and result in long term problems. If the market eventually recovers, it can take years for your retirement to pick up again.

7. Goal related risk

Here, this is a risk of not having enough retirement funds to spend. As you will have a particular lifestyle to fund, there's a risk of running out of money to continue living the way you want.

HOW TO HANDLE INVESTMENT RISKS

Many investors get carried away by the idea of investing for retirement to the point that they ignore proper management of risks associated with investing. They don't know how to time the market. They invest during buying seasons and sell when they are supposed to buy.

Risks form a part of investment. And knowing how to handle risk can go a long way in securing your retirement future. For that, you need to formulate solid offense strategies which will protect you while you invest.

Your investing offense span across different approaches. You can choose to buy into stock options of companies outperforming themselves. Or you could use select undervalued stocks, give them time to reach a desired price before investing your money. All in all, you want your money to grow and appreciate in value.

While having a strategy for increasing your money feels great, you also need to have a defense strategy. Your defense strategy serves as a cushion pending when your investments do not go according to plan. It is a system set to reduce risks and offer protection for your money in those down times.

To properly handle investment risks and their potential negative effects:

1. Invest in inflation friendly investments

You can choose to invest in real estate or stock shares that grow with inflation. You can also buy bonds together with Treasury Inflation-Protected Securities which offer you returns depending on the rate of inflation.

With this, even the inflation increases, you are duly compensated for it.

2. Employ diversification

Diversifying means mixing different investments in a portfolio. This is a risk managem-ent strategy where you invest in diverse asset types and investments to decrease risk. Like the saying goes, Place not all your eggs into one basket. Diversifying prevents your assets from being heavily dependent on one sector. That way, if one investment falls through, other assets back it up.

Possessing a single stock option exposes you to the poor management that may occur in the company you purchased from. You can reduce this risk by buying stock options from different sectors or purchasing index funds which holds diverse stocks.

Asset allocation can be helpful in reducing risks yet there is no guarantee in the results of a diversified portfolio can produce. Note that before you diversify, you need to understand the pros and cons of each asset class.

3. Be a calculated risk-taker

In the game of investing, spontaneity is disastrous. You must take calculated steps in ensuring your money is placed in an investment with guaranteed returns. You need to know when to act and vice versa. Like the Boys Scout motto, 'Always Be Prepared', you must have available cash pending when good opportunity to invest open up. You can do this by building an opportunity fund. Your opportunity fund allows you to cash in on investment opportunities when they appear.

To employ this strategy of calculated risk-taking, you need to be up to date on the workings of the investment you are targeting. Do plenty of research, learn to evaluate the market logically and rationally (avoid emotional investments, they always fail) and assess the market using certain indicators such as the P/E ratio and yield curve. Always apply the good old common sense when investing.

4. Insure the investment results

You can also handle investment risk by insuring against it. If you are using the traditional insurance types like home or car insurance, you will need to pay a premium that will cover certain losses. Investment insurance applies the same tactic. You purchase an annuity that will pay you an income for life.

An annuity is of two types; a fixed annuity and a variable annuity. An annuity is not an investment but an insurance product that reduces your investment risk. Because it is tax deferred, you can use it to defer taxes on your investments and generate more money for your retirement.

5. Rebalance

You can manage risk by selling out stock investments or assets that occupy too much space in your investment portfolio. Many long-term investors use this approach. After selling those assets, they will now buy stocks options and other asset types that are underperforming.

6. Avoid all risks

This is the best means of handling investment risk- avoid risks. You can avoid risks by investing in safe retirement investments with guaranteed outcomes. In fact, avoiding risk is a smart to do when investing money. With that, you can acquire more skills useful in risk management.

Ensure to avoid risk on money you will need in a short time you will want that money completely available to you. This is known as emergency funds or reserve assets. The return on this investment type is usually low, but that is the cost of having your money safe and guaranteed. It is wise to have reserve funds before taking on more risky investments

CHAPTER 4

HOW TO WORK FOR EARLY RETIREMENT

It is one thing to work and it's another to work in a job that can help you achieve your early retirement goals. Even if you work in a job you love, fantasies of leaving for a work free lifestyle will crop up. It is important your job is not only paying your bills, but preparing you for the lifestyle you aim to live after retiring. If your job is not favorable, you may need to change jobs or get a supplement income source.

A study by GoBankingRates found out that hundreds of Americans will continue to work past 65 years due to factors such as outliving their retirement funds, limited wages or working at jobs without the guarantee of retirement income.

Despite that, there are many jobs that can boost your chances at retiring early compared to others.

POSSIBLE JOBS THAT WILL ALLOW YOU TO RETIRE EARLY

The following jobs were outlined by GoBankingRates as the best jobs for those seeing early retirement and wealth.

1. Mechanical engineers

The Elon Musks are on this list. Mechanical engineers are paid higher salaries, with an average of $91500 on a yearly basis. As they are paid more, they can put in the extra money into a retirement plan.

2. Insurance jobs

On an average, ten percentage of those who will work past 65 years is 37.9%. Those who work as insurance sales men or women can afford to contribute $2.47 on an hourly basis to their 401k.

3. Early school educators

61% of kindergarten school teachers aim to retire on or before 62 years. This occupation is noted to have the fourth highest percentage of employees who want to retire early. These teachers are financially confident they will retire early.

4. Psychologists

Less than one third of psychologists work beyond 65 years. On an average, 27.8% plan to work beyond age 65 leaving the others as early retirees.

5. Industrial engineers

The industrial engineer earns a significant annual income of $90000. Most of the engineers make 3%

contributions to their 401k which are matched by their employer by 50%. By age 62, many of them will have over $500000 saved for retirement.

6. Special education teachers

66% of these teachers aim to retire early, while the others aim to work beyond 62 years.

7. Computer programmers and administrators

Tech is a highly lucrative industry. A whopping 56% aim to retire early.

8. Financial sales operations

Financial sales workers often make almost six figures on an average. Because of the high salaries associated with this job type, it is easy to create a large nest egg for retirement.

9. Physical scientists

Many physical scientists desire to retire before 62 years. Based on survey, 27% still want to work beyond 62 years' this job has people who are more likely to retire early because of the financial standing surrounding this job.

10. Firefighting jobs

Workers in this industry enjoy great retirement benefits. The hourly contribution made to the employee's account is $5.83.

11. Lawyers and judges

People in this position enjoy huge salaries and re estimated to retire before 62 years.

12. Aircraft mechanics

Hourly contributions made by employers to 401k for this jib type is $5.13 on an average.

13. Pharmacists

Pharmacists earn an average of $121,700 on a yearly basis. Because of the financial benefits they enjoy, they are rated the second highest to retire before 62 years.

14. Pilots

Pilots and people within the aviation industry are noted to be the topmost people to retire early given the estimated average annual wage of $138000. They are also recorded to have high 401k contributions which allows them to retire early.

15. Dentists

Dentists are noted to have saved over a million dollars in their retirement account because of the huge financial benefits associated with this job type.

HOW EARLY RETIREMENT OPENS YOUR EYES TO NEW OPPORTUNITIES

When you are retired, you have more time to observe the world around you. This is because you are not neck deep in the hustle and bustle of your work and life activities.

When you retire early, you will see that living static is not an option. Things will definitely change but you will set the rules and live as you want. Retiring comes with a lot of freedom. You get to decide what to do with the freedom so you can live your best life.

This is a time when you matter. Trying to please someone else holds no relevance. You choose the activities that you will enjoy and the impact that they have on you and your environment.

You get the opportunity to travel the world or to go to that place or city you have always wanted. You could choose to explore the city you have always lived in. Either way, you get to experience new cultures and environments and gain new experiences.

You left a job with a steady income. Retiring doesn't mean the end of work. Instead, retiring gives you the opportunity to work again. You can choose to become your own boss. You could turn a hobby into a full-time business. You could get a side hustle, freelance work as a consultant for a company.

You can even decide not to retire but to take a sabbatical. That brief break for work allows you to enjoy retirement perks without leaving the workforce. Sabbatical can be one week one months, some months, a year or two.

Another opportunity that comes with retiring early is the freedom to live wherever you want. You can choose to relocate and start life afresh in a new environment. You can choose to rent a vacation home or even do a house swap. A house swap allows you to live in a home you desire while the owner lives in your home too. You trade your homes for a brief period. That way, you have a feel of a new home or environment.

Retirement is also an opportunity to write your own book. You have many life experiences to document and this is the time to out those ideas down. You don't need a formal education to write a book. You also choose the way you want to publish it? Will you self-publish or go through the traditional way?

You will have to understand that being old has nothing to do with your age. You could be 70 years with the energy and vigor of a 20 years old.

You can also choose to maintain your retirement plan. Since you have no steady income, it is essential to do a financial assessment of your money on a periodic basis.

Retiring provides myriad opportunities to delve into many pursuits. This is the time of your life to explore and truly live the life you deserve.

CHAPTER 5

HOW TO CREATE A WORK LIFE BALANCE THAT GUARANTEES EARLY RETIREMENT

It is possible to spend ample time juggling work duties while taking care of your family. But when planning your retirement, you will have to create a new routine. Changing your life for retirement can be difficult. The thought of following your longtime passions and hobbies and spending quality time without the hassle of a work environment can be blissful but getting into retirement changes the routine you are used to.

So, how to you create a work life balance that ensure you ease into retirement a comfortable way? Have a plan. Most of the time, being in a work environment bolsters the feeling of productivity. We are able to interact with people on a daily basis. So those getting on the retirement plan can make one feel lost and without purpose. That is why you need to have a plan.

1. Gradually ease out of work

If you possibly can, reduce your workdays or the number of hours you work. You can choose to be more flexible by freelancing. This will allow you to adjust to a different lifestyle, and you will not feel jarred when you leave your workplace finally.

2. Know the activities you will engage in once you retire

While it is liberating to be free from your alarm and work pressure, you may lose your wits if you don't have activities to engage you. Think of what you want to do to occupy yourself. Do you want to take up a new skill, volunteer or get another degree? Do you want to turn a passion into a business or work as a freelancer?

3. Connect to others

Retiring can get pretty emotional. You will be leaving a familiar environment and people you are bonded with for a long time. By retiring, you will feel you have lost them. Instead of letting go completely, create meetup times with them. Make use of social media to keep the connections going. Also, make new friends, build new relationships and maintain the old and the new. It will help life exciting and fun.

4. Sort out your finances

It will be terrible to go into retirement with debts. How about honing your skill in budgeting? You will need that during your retirement years since you don't have a regular income.

ACHIEVING EARLY RETIREMENT SUCCESS THROUGH INVESTMENT

You already know that investing is an important element to retire early. To excel at investing, you have to learn to think and act as an investor. You need to develop the mindset associated with investing. Then out into practice what you know. Investing may deal with numbers but it is more of an art and common sense. In all, proper management of your money holds more importance that the investments you made.

In this present age, the investing game has changed. Before anything else, you need to save in a tax advantaged plan like the IRA or 401k. then, you may include the Roth ira and leave the money to compound until you are ready to retire.

By deciding to retire early, you have taken a risk. You are giving up years of your life that you could have earned more. So, you must depend on what you have saved, and the returns it compounded to support you for a lifetime. If you outlive it, you lose big time. So, when investing, you don't need risky ventures for this. There is no guarantee that leaving your money in a stock market will provide good enough income you can lie on. in fact, anything regarding investing is not guaranteed but there are smart strategies you can employ to better your retirement funds.

The least investment plan often revolves around index funds and mutual funds. There are many more investments you can get involve in for early retirement as you will read in the next chapter.

POSSIBLE INVESTMENT PLANS TO CONSIDER DURING EARLY RETIREMENT

Some of the best investments you can indulge in to boost your retirement are:

1. CDs

CDs or Certificates of Deposits are usually governed by banks. They provide a much higher interest rate compared to savings accounts. CDs are given time to mature. Their maturity dates could span from week to months or even years. During that period, you will not be allowed to withdraw. If you must withdraw, you will be penalized.

Interest on CDs are paid at intervals. At the time of maturity, both capital and interests are returned to you. Do you due diligence to know the best rates.

This safe investment is an ideal choice for retirees who want their money locked up for some time. Note that there are different types of CDs to cater for different needs.

While CDs are generally safe, they possess certain risks especially when it comes to reinvestment or increased rates. To reduce this, ladder your CDs, that is, invest your money in a variety of CDs so that your money will not be constrained to only one investment. This is because taxes and inflation can drastically reduce the purchasing power of your cd.

Unlike a savings accounts, CDs has no liquidity. They are time deposits and cannot be withdrawn from until maturity date. Getting your money sooner will cost you a penalty.

2. High yield savings accounts

These are easy to access. Compared to your local savings accounts, online banks provide higher interest at little costs. You have total access to your money by simply doing a money transfer or withdrawing via an atm. This account is ideal for those who need cash soon enough.

There is no fear of losing your money since the accounts are insured by FDIC. They are also safe investments, but you can earn less when you reinvest because of the inflation. While you have access to your money anytime, the number of withdrawals you can make per day is determined by your bank.

3. Short term corporate bonds

Many corporations often issue bonds to investors. These bonds are presented as bond funds which contain bonds many corporations give. These bonds have a maturity period of at least one year and five years at most. Because of this, they are less affected by inflation and fluctuations in interest rates compared to longs term bonds.

Corporate bonds funds are ideal for retirees who need cash flow. You can also take advantage of this if you want to reduce your portfolio risk while making returns.

Despite its ideal nature, corporate bond funds are not FDIC insured. Companies that offer them may experience low credit rating and defer on those bonds as a result. To limit this, ensure to purchase high quality bonds.

Your bonds can be resold or bought every business day. You can also reinvest the returns or carry out added investments whenever you wish. However, note that losses are a part of it.

4. Government bond funds

These are ETFs invested in debt security by the Unites states and its corresponding agencies. The funds are invested in debt instruments like t-bonds, t-notes, T-bills all issued by enterprise that are sponsored by the government. These funds are ideal for investors with conservative risk.

While these bonds are regarded as the safest because they are in the care of the Us government, the funds itself have no government backing. This means that the funds can be affected by market volatility. Inflation and interest rate fluctuations can decrease the prices and quality of these funds despite their liquid nature.

5. Dividend stock funds

Stocks that pay dividends can make your stock investments much safer. A dividend is a portion of the profit a company's makes and pays to its shareholder on a periodic basis. A dividend stock allows you gain more on your investment in the long run. These are best suited for experienced investors.

These set of funds have a safe appeal, but not without risks. It is smarter to invest in companies with a record of increase in dividend instead of those ranking with the highest yields.

These funds can be bought or sold on market days and the periodic pays can be liquidated. You can see a better performance of your investment over long term period.

Reinvesting your dividends is a good idea for higher returns.

6. S&P 500 index funds

If you still have many years ahead to retiree or you want a g-higher return, you can select this option. These funds come from a lot of successful American companies like Amazon or instance.

The S&P 500 index funds provides diversification which means you can own a part of hundreds of these companies at the same time. This is because the funds comprise companies across all industries. They make the best and most resilient funds which you can get a low cost. This fund is ideal for starting investors and early retirement savers.

While it offers little risks in terms of investing in stocks, it is still of a volatile nature because it involves stocks. Also, it is not insured by the government s it can be affected by market changes.

This fund can be liquidated on market days.

7. Municipal bond funds

These funds invest in diverse municipal munis or bonds which are issued by either the state or the local government or both. Interest accrued on these funds are tax free federally, and sometimes state and locally too.

You can buy a municipal bond individually or via mutual or exchange traded fund. Get the support of a financial adviser. Buy bonds related to your state or locality to enjoy more in terms of taxes as well.

For your retirement, these funds provide good cash flow which you can plough into your retirement plan. It offers you diverse bonds and saves you the time of analyzing each bond.

However, these bonds can be defaulted. While municipal bonds are generally safe, economic volatility in your state or local government may affect payment.

Also, bonds are sometimes callable. Your issuer can return the principal and default on the bond before it matures, thereby making you lose out on the interests it had accrued.

You are allowed to liquidate your bond funds on business days. You can also reinvest or increase your investments when you want it.

8. Nasdaq-100 index funds

Index funds on Nasdaq-100 is an excellence option if you want to invest in the biggest and most successful tech companies without having to analyze those companies. This fund relies on Nasdaq's 100 finest companies. So, they select the most stable and powerful companies like Microsoft and Facebook.

These funds allow you to diversify and protects you from investing in any downside of any of the companies. The best pf the index funds offer low expenses. This means, they provide ana affordable means for you to own the companies.

On the flip side, these stocks can collapse as well. Usually, Nasdaq houses the best tech giants that are valued highly. Just as highly valued as they are, they can also experience a downfall in hard time.

These funds are easy to liquidate on the days market opens.

9. Rentals

If you want to manage properties, thus is a great investment for you. Currently, mortgage rates are lower than ever; you may take advantage by getting yourself your own property.

If you will be investing in rentals, it is smart to select the right property, buy it, manage it well and handle tenants. Smart purchases will help you in the long run. Unlike other investments, you cannot buy rentals from a tap of the button on your phone. You may even be disturbed at odd hours over an unsatisfactory part of your property like a plumbing problem.

Overtime, your assets can accumulate in value, helping you to clear debts, increase you rents and produce cash flow before you retire.

On the flip side, you can pay too much for a house. Even with the interest rates falling low and limited supply of homes, the prices of properties increased in 2020 admitting the global struggle. Unlike other assets, you cannot easily liquidate your property.

That means, if you want some quick cash, getting a property may not be the ideal option. Plus, your broker can have up to 6% commission off the sales of your property.

CHAPTER 6

HOW TO DISCOVER POSSIBLE INVESTMENT OPPORTUNITIES AFTER EARLY RETIREMENT

Just because you are retired doesn't mean you cannot continue to invest. As we have earlier established, saving and investing are lifelong habits. Habits you must establish to keep the money coming in whether you work or not.

So, while you are enjoying that well-deserved vacation or following your longtime passion, you must still lookout for ways to create wealth and keep the cash flow coming in. you don't want to outlive your savings, so investing in money making assets is the way to go.

So, how do you go about finding what's new in the investment market?

Invest in alternative markets.

Here you have to be cautious though. Yu retirement funds can easily get lost yet can provide amazing returns if well handled. Alternative markets are relatively new and are constantly evolving. If you want to be limited by the already known routes lie stocks or bonds, you can consider these opportunities.

Seek out experienced investors

Hey, you are not a know it all. Sometimes, you may have exhausted the options you had for investment opportunities and don't know where to begin. You also may not have the time to research the market, or you may be too busy with life to care. Getting an experienced and up to date investor is a great option. Rather than rely on the internet or online forums, having someone in real life who has a nose for investment will keep you in the loop and help you maximize those opportunities as well.

Watch the news

If you want to know where money is, watch the news. Keeping a tab on the global financial news is important to stay abreast of the happenings in the financial world. While you will not want to jump on every trend, knowing what's going on out there will help you recognize opportunities you may not be aware of.

MAKING YOUR SAVING WORK FOR YOU AFTER SERVICE

There are many investment opportunities you can take advantage of after you have retired. Although it is not set in stone, the following are ideal options you can make use of to get your hard-earned savings working for you. The aim is to extend your savings and gain more freedom to enjoy retirement and keep up the lifestyle of your dreams.

Invest in cash

One investment a retiree you should consider is cash investment. You need money to handle the daily expenses and keep up with necessities like the food and rent. Also, handy cash is required for those vacations you have dreamt of taking.

Even if you have available cash, it's not prudent to leave them in an account where they are not accruing in interest. Rather, plough a portion of your money into money market account. You can also put your money into a savings account that has a high interest rate. By doing this, you will have available cash which is still working for you.

Invest in bonds

Bonds are conservative investments, meaning you should not expect high returns. Yet they provide a way for your money to grow at a steady pace. They might not have been attractive to you in your youth but once you are retired, it is important to protect your money. At this stage, you cannot afford to gamble with your money and there's even less time to gain lost money back at this stage.

A bond ladder is a common option many retirees use. Buying a bond ladder allows you to buy a variety of bonds with timely maturity rates. As the bonds mature, you will expect to receive steady cash consecutively instead of a huge payout at a go.

You can also invest in mutual bond fund, these bonds also let you invest in diverse bonds. You can expect steady income and have your investments handled by professionals.

Invest in stocks

Ok, so stocks are riskier and generally thought to be more ideal when you were younger. However, as a retiree, you can include this as a part of your investing strategy. Although you want to invest in more conservative investments as you age, but a small portion of your income should be in stocks. This must be doe according to your financial situation and risk level.

It is essential to select the correct stocks. Chasing big returns from stocks in tech is more ideal for younger investors. Rather as a retiree, select stocks with a slow yet steady rates which also provide dividends. All of which must get money into your pocket.

BEST INVESTMENT OPPORTUNITIES NO ONE IS TALKING ABOUT

When you talk about investing, stocks and mutual funds often come to mind. these and many others have had their trumpets blown long enough that you may not think many other options exists. But with the ever-changing stock market and the plunging interest rates, many other interesting investing opportunities have sprung up. As exciting as they are, one must exercise caution when investing in these. A rule of thumb would be to have 5-15% of your portfolio in these investments.

1. Music royalties

There are songs out there produces $10000 or more on an average every year. You can purchase a song and earn from them. Many songwriters offer a part of their royalties for sale on online websites such as TheRoyaltyExchange.com. after purchasing the song, you will be receiving royalties until the expiration of the copyright.

2. Tax lien certificates

Due to the tight economy, man homeowners have been cash trapped and unable to pay taxes on their properties. Now investors are utilizing this opportunity to buy tax lien. You can do this because the local governments dislike waiting for the tax ills. Rather they sell tax liens at an auction where investors prefer high rate with low risk. On benefit of this is that the interest penalty comes up a day after purchasing he lien. That way, investors earn interest no matter when the lien is repaid.

3. Bank account bonuses

Currently, the Bank of America is coming up with new ways to charge their customers. Meanwhile, a couple of banks pay huge bonuses to new account holders. Using bank bonuses, you can make money fast and accumulate high returns in a short time.

4. eBay land

eBay is one of the biggest online marketplaces and is also known for the land auction it runs which is incredibly cheap. The plots are cheap because of low demand and the unattractive locations. Still, many investors buy into this in the hope that those lands gain value someday. This is a gamble though.

5. Fine art

When it comes to art, the truly wealthy are the kings. But now, an average person can cash it on some high-quality paintings. Masterworks is a company that gathers funds from people to purchase artworks regarded as blue chip. It claims to offer at least 10% annual returns. You can consider this option if you want a creative way to scale the market.

6. Gold

Valuable metals like gold are in short supply because less and less are being mined. Because of that there are numerous opportunities available to give you cash in exchange for your gold. Most times precious metals like silver, gold, jewels are free of money. regardless of the fluctuating dollar, gold is consistent and will continue to be extravagant.

Gold is useful in terms of financial problems. Then you can exchange your gold during emergencies and buy it back when you are financially buoyant. Based on history, the rich usually kept their money in gold bars.

CHAPTER 7

BENEFITS OF EARLY RETIREMENT

Retiring early sets you apart for more enjoyment of life. You will get to explore more of your passions and interests you wouldn't have had time for when working.

PROS AND CONS OF EARLY RETIREMENT

Consider the following pros if you are thinking of retiring early:

1. More active years

If you retire early and young, you have more active years to enjoy the lifestyle of your dreams. You can travel the world, take up a new sport, or take better care of your health, while keeping your expenses low.

2. It's the perfect time

You've worked hard enough, beaten challenges to the dust and achieved milestones. You deserve a break, some time for yourself and retiring early is the best way to do that. After you have retired, you have the freedom to create the desired lifestyle that produces immense joy and satisfaction for you.

3. It helps you become healthier

Being away from the office pressure can be a health booster for you. In fact, you are more likely to get healthier when out of the hustle and bustle of the workplace. A study conducted in 2002 on British Civil workers showed that those who retired at age 60, especially those with high-ranking jobs recorded tremendous improvement in their health because they weren't subjected to work stress.

4. It helps you to begin another career

If you wish to switch careers or begin a business, retiring early affords you ample time for that. If you are getting set for a new career, you may be a more ideal candidate tom potential employees because of the wealth and experience you have gathered.

On the other hand, if you want to turn your passion into a business, you will have sufficient time to build and nurture your dream business. That will keep your mind in top mental state for a couple more years.

THE CONS OF RETIRING EARLY INCLUDE;

1. Lesser benefits of Social Security

When you are retired early, you are allowed to cash in on your social security. Unfortunately, your benefits will be much smaller compared to when you retire at the eligible age of 67. In fact, your benefits will be 30% lower.

2. Work embodies you

You may be planning to retire but giving up work is not part of your plan, especially if you are either a workaholic or you have a deep love for work. That aside, work forms an essential part of our lives. As human beings we must constantly be in action.

You may have started work as a teenager or young adult. From making money to attaining certain luxuries, work for you may have evolved into something more meaningful, such as creating a role and identity for you in society.

The American society is such that your work and title define your value and worth before others. So, retiring early can create that identity problem and you may find yourself answering I'm retired in social networking gatherings.

3. You will be nostalgic about your previous colleagues

Retiring early means giving up a whole lot; From the stress and bumps of you 9-5, the routines and the relationships you have created. Working plays a vital role in your life. It makes you purposeful while providing you the security of a destination- your workplace. So, when you retire, you will feel a sense of freedom and cater on, a sense of loss of the bustle of your workplace. And you will miss it.

4. You desire to be up to date

You may not want to retire early. While an early retirement can be attractive, you may still want to be on top of the happenings within your industry. Of course, you want the relaxation an early retirement brings, but you refuse to lose your relevance and networks when you retire.

WHEN TO INVEST AFTER RETIREMENT

Even after you have retired, you should not stop saving or investing. In fact, saving and investing are two financial habits that must remain constant even if you have amassed wealth to last you a lifetime. They are the two lifelines guaranteed to keep your money ever growing.

By continuously investing, you are being financially proactive and increasing your financial freedom and purchasing power even if you are well beyond working age.

CHAPTER 8

HOW GOOD FINANCIAL PLANS CAN INFLUENCE YOUR INVESTMENT DECISIONS

A financial plan is a life process of creating smart goals, with specific dollar amounts and knowing how to move from one point to another. How to mostly, financial planning is not focused or money or investing. It is about turning your dreams into the reality of the lifestyle you want to for yourself when you retire. It is about allowing to save, invest and still life the way you desire.

Financial planning will teach you patience as your plan works for you. You will not be hasty in putting your money in any investment because you will consider your goals. It brings to your awareness your desired financial outcome so that when making a financial decision, you will cross check it with those goals and not make a decision you are bound to regret.

Financial planning will teach you discipline, to stick with the plan no matter what. It also helps you embody the habits that will take you to the success you desire and keep you in it.

Know your net worth

To know your net worth, first and foremost, determine your assets. These assets can be converted to cash. Examples of assets include CDs, savings accounts, money market accounts and so on.

Create a list of your lifestyle assets. These are things you make use of on a daily basis. They are a part of you. You may have bought them or were gifted them. Get their prices and put them down. If you cannot get their prices, make an estimate. Examples include jewelry, property, valuables, cars and trucks etc.

Add the account statements to know the assets you have invested. Some of them are bonds, stocks, partnerships and so on.

Write down all your liabilities. Your liabilities include mortgage, credit cards, taxes, bills, credit card loans etc. Out down all the thins you owe. After that minus the liabilities from your assets. If your net worth is positive, that means you are in a good financial position. But if your net worth is a negative number, that means you owe beyond what you are worth.

KNOWING WHEN TO CONSULT AN EXPERT

To consult an expert or not to consult? That decision is totally up to you.

Some people believe you should meet with a financial expert who can help you pick and handle stock investments. Or any other type of investments. On the flip side, others believe one should manage one's own investments.

Before deciding to hire a consultant or not, ask yourself these two questions:

1. What is your level of knowledge on investing and financial planning? If you know little on these areas, hiring the services of a financial expert will be useful to you. The expert will help you grow and make better financial decisions, they will also help you select investments that will help you achieve your goals.

2. Do you have the time to spare to manage your investments? You may be knowledge-able about investments. Heck! You have done one or three in your time; however, you may have too little time to advise yourself financially. Investing ad financial planning are time consuming.

3. So, before you seek an expert, know the certifications and level of experience he or she possesses when it comes to financial management. Interview potential financial experts before you hire any. At times, the length of years (experience)

is not a determinant for effective management of your money or making sound financial decisions.

4. Whoever you want to hire must confidently list references who can acknowledge his performance. If this is not the case, you can look for other experts.

THE DIFFERENT FINANCIAL PLANNERS

1. Enrolled Agent (EA)

This position is controlled by the IRS. The individual would have excelled in tests regarding taxation. If not, the individual must have at least five years of experience in a technical position. This position allows the individual to stand in for taxpayers in court.

2. Chartered financial consultant

The position is the financial planning position of the insurance industry. The consultants must meet the requirements for experience. they must have also passed exams relating to finance and investment.

3. Chartered financial analyst

This position is given by the institute of chartered financial analysts. This is awarded to analysts who are experienced and who have excelled in exams relating to financial accounting, security analysis, portfolio management etc.

4. Certified public accountant

This accountant is experienced and have met the requirement in the statutory, educational and licensing aspects at the location of the practice.

5. Chartered life underwriter

This position is awarded to individuals who have business experience in areas regarding insurance planning. The individual must also have passed examinations regarding insurance and similar subjects.

Some questions you could ask your potential expert are:

1. What is your educational background? What schools did you attend and what degrees have you acquired?
2. Do you have a license form the state securities division?
3. Did you register with securities and exchange commission?
4. Have you been given the license to sell financial products?
5. Are you a representative for any financial company?
6. Is the expert fee based or fee only? If he is fee only, that means he will charge you a fee ion an annual basis to manage your investment account. If he is fee based, he will get paid a commission on the products he sells.
7. What is your annual fee as a fee only expert?
8. Can you provide a reference list? This will help you gauge the expert's actual performance.
9. What is you background in the financial world?
10. What professional certifications do you have?

11. What are the limits to the services you will provide for the fee I will pay you?
12. Will you give my money to a third party to manage?
13. How do you help clients make good investment decisions based on their financial needs?
14. Who are your target clients?

Interviewing many advisers and asking questions such as these provides clarity in your relationship whoever you will hire as well as ease any concern you have. Also note, that the cost of hiring an expert differs from the fees and expenses you will have to pay on your investments.

On roboadvisers

A roboadviser is someone who does not allow you to fully manage your investments, yet does not offer you total help many investors need. Roboadvisers are common among investors who want to reduce fees that come with managing investments while increasing wealth. If you don't want to make use of the traditional investment firm, you can hire a roboadviser.

MISTAKE TO AVOID WHEN HIRING A FINANCIAL EXPERT

1. Don't hire the first person you meet

It may be tempting to hire he first person that falls on your list or indicate interest. Doing so may be costly. Give yourself time. Interview a couple of experts before you hire any.

2. Don't hire an advisor who isn't a fiduciary

A fiduciary is a person who is bound to ethically act in the best interests of another. This removes any conflicting interest and increases the integrity of the expert's advice.

3. Don't select an expert with the wrong niche

Every financial expert has his or her own area of specialty. You need to know the specialty of the advisor before hiring and make sure it aligns with you needs. Also, know the strengths and weaknesses of the advisor.

4. don't hire without seeing the credentials of the expert

before an expert can give you advice, they have gone through a series of tests. Request licensees and credentials before hiring one.

5. Don't hire an expert on your own

Hiring an expert can be a difficult task because there are many high-quality experts.

6. Don't hire an expert whose payment process is difficult to understand

Financial advisors are paid in different ways. Some charge you flat rates outrightly, some charge a portion of your assets. Also ensure your advisor is not earning off you while ignoring your interests.

7. Don't hire an advisor without a compatible strategy

Every expert has a personalized strategy. That's what made him or her stand out. Some may advise investing in conservative investments, others in aggressive instruments. If you prefer mutual funds, choosing an expert who loves index funds is not a good option.

METHODS OF MAKING MONEY

You need to know how the financial planner makes his money. There are generally three ways by which this happens:

1. Fee based- that is the planner charges on an hourly or quarterly basis.

2. Commission based-this means the planners create basic financial plans, offer financial advice, and offer financial products or services.

3. Fee and commission based-this means that the planner would charge on an hourly basis or a flat fee as well as offer products or service that will help you accomplish your financial plan.

CHAPTER 9

BUDGETING FOR YOUR EARLY RETIREMENT INVESTMENT

Having successful retirement requires a budget. You need a budget to effectively handle your income and expenses. Most of the time, people are spooked by the idea of a budget because they associate it with living a restrictive life. They want to limit themselves by limiting how they spend money. In reality, budgeting gives you freedom. It gets rid of erroneous spending that will derail you from your financial goals. It also pushes you towards your financial freedom faster.

Have you ever received your paycheck only to find yourself with almost nothing by the second week of the following month? Have you found yourself wondering where your money goes? Have you ever felt like you just never have enough even when you have just received a paycheck?

You see, knowing the direction your money is taking will help you in retiring early. But if you cannot control your money, you will waste your money on expenses you ate far better without.

HOW TO BUILD A BUDGET

Building a budget is easy. Using a sheet of paper and a pen, or a spreadsheet document. Draw a line dividing the paper in two. On the left side, label it the income column. Put down he total money you receive after tax from every income source. Your income source is not limited to your paycheck. You can receive money from your investments, business and interests accrued on savings.

On the right side of the column, label it expenses column. Write down all the things you spend money on every month. Now create a monthly budget for the things you hardly buy per month. If you don't know how to go about this, you are kook at you bank and credit card statement for the past twelve months. This will reveal additional expenses you may not have taken note off.

Also, allocate money for splurges, emergenc-ies and your savings as well.

After creating your budget, look at the numbers. Are you expenses higher than your income or vice versa? Do you have left over money every month? Leftover money is the surplus you have over month.

Many people tend to overspend. That way they accumulate more debt than they intend. If you budget shows a deficit, you have to start cutting expenses. If those expenses cannot be reduced, you need to get an additional income source so that you will have surplus by the end of the month.

ON REDUCING EXPENSES

One reason many people record deficits in their budgets is because they spend on wants which leaves a gaping hole in their pockets. They cannot differentiate between a want and a need. A need is that which you cannot live without. This includes food, shelter, clothing, heath etc. A want is what you can do without. Sometimes a need can become a want, for instance, food is a need but eating out is a want.

By having a clear understanding of needs and wants, you will be able to focus on your needs and define spending on wants so that you can build the wealth needed for you to retire early.

Even after creating your budget, ensure to refine it as often as you can. Look for ways to reduce spending on both needs and wants. Look at your needs and wants with your spouse or an accountability partner. Your accountability partner must be a financial prudent person, not a spender like yourself. Evaluate which item on the needs and wants list can be sacrificed for you to retire early.

As you are evaluating your wants and needs, you can begin with wants. Wants are the easiest because they involve things you can do without. Try challenging yourself to eliminate as much as possible. See when you are downsizing, look for better options you can use instead. Look at the needs list as well. Note the areas where you can get cheaper yet better quality options.

Most of the time, the biggest expense is your home. You can reduce expenses on your home by rightsizing. Right sizing means getting the right house for your needs so you will not have to spend much. Another way to right size is to move to another area where the cost of moving is low. To do this requires planning, and you will need to consider the factors such as finances and emotions among others. If moving out is not an option, you could rent out a spare bedroom or storage space.

Every expense you can remove or reduce will go a lot way in helping you reach financial freedom and become wealthy enough to retire. Now this doesn't mean you will have to live like a monk. Rather budgeting allows you to prioritize what is of essence to you.

WAYS OF REDUCING EXPENSES

The cash system

Expenses like food, gasoline, entertainment fluctuate on every now and then. They can take a lot of money out of you if you are not paying attention. To deal with this, you can make use of cash payment system. The cash payment system stops you from spending beyond your budget.

To use this system, get an envelope for every cash payment system you have. That is if you spend $500 on groceries, put $500 into the envelope for groceries per month. When you want to spend in that area, make use of the cash in that envelope. Whenever the money is that envelope is exhausted, you have spent the budget in that area for that month. If you need you spend more, you will have to take out cash from another envelope which in turn reduces the budget in that area.

Using debit cards

If carrying cash abut is uncomfortable for you, make use of prepaid debit cards. These cards are available at big box stores. Similar to the cash system, you load the amount you are spending in an area for the month. When spending, the card is used to make payments.

Note that the cards come with fees and an expiration date. Sometimes, the issuers charge recurring fees. So before getting card, shop for the no fees cards. Pay attention to the expiration dates. If the car expires while money is still inside, you may not recover it.

Budgeting apps

If the previous options are not ideal for you, you can use budgeting apps. The internet is filled with many great budgeting apps you can use.

Mvelopes is one of them. This app allows you to divide pending expenses into different online envelopes. The envelopes ensure you have enough money to pay the usual monthly bills. It also keeps track of the amount you are spending in areas like groceries transportation and the likes.

You have the option of linking the app with your bank account, but you can decide not to do that. But doing so will allow for easier use of the system so you won't have to manually input every expense you make. A great thing to note about this app is that it used encrypted to protect your financial details. This app has three versions you can use: the free version, Premier version and the Coaching version each with their unique features.

Another great budgeting app is Good budget. It is similar to the envelope system as well but the virtual kind. You can create savings goals, synchronize the information in a way that you can share with someone else. This app runs two versions. They are the free and the Plus versions. It also presents a pictorial representation of your spending using a pie chart.

You can also make use of a spreadsheet to create and track your budget but these apps among others make budgeting easier and faster. Despite the ease of use, you need discipline to ensure that you will not exceed the amount you have dedicated to each area.

It is discipline that allows you to effectively use the money you set aside for investing so as to speed up your financial freedom.

Surplus is the key

The key to creating a budget that helps you build wealth fast is having a good amount of money remaining by month end. In fact, when you reduce your expense, you tend to accumulate more money when the month ends.

Retiring early requires that you keep track of every dollar and be prudent in every money action you take. You need to know that whatever you spend money on affects you in the long run, so spending on frivolity adds little value to your life and reduces your chances of retiring early.

HOW TO FINANCE AN INVESTMENT PLAN

Financing an investment plan simply means putting money into your investments. you must have enough funds to invest so that you can achieve your investment goals. Where will this money come from? If you are working in a 9-5, you already have a steady income source from which you can divert a portion into your investments. However, chances are your salary is barely enough to cover your expenses, so you have to seek more ways to increase your money so that you can put in more money into your investments while catering to our expenses.

Increasing your income

Making just the minimum wage is barely enough for you to achieve financial independence and retire early. Since it is already difficult to save money, you need to seek out ways to multiply your money. Look out for avenues and opportunities aligned to your interests that you can gain more money from.

Increase your money from your present jobs

Look out for ways you can make more money from your job. Does it involve you working overtime? Can you apply for a higher position or increase in pay? You will need to discuss with your boss on ways you can add more value to the company while increasing your money. Discuss with your boss on ways you could advance further in the company. You could let your boss know the extra efforts you are outing in the company and let him or her know why you deserve higher pay.

Take an extra job

If getting higher raise from your current place of work is not forthcoming, you can take up an extra job in another company. You could get hired part time for a position similar to what you are doing or one that aligns with your interests. You can decide t work evenings or weekends. Whatever time you choose, ensure the extra funds come in. also decide on your income goal. The extra job you are doing is temporary. It is to supplement your goal.

Get a side hustle

You don't need to own your own business. You could work for yourself in a side hustle. Your side hustle could be a skill you are great at. You could manage other peoples' businesses, work as a freelancer among others.

LEARNING MORE ABOUT THE BEST COMPANIES TO INVEST IN

Investing in a company can be daunting especially when you can see so many available options. If you are a beginner, looking at the stock market to get shares of public companies isn't always helpful or beneficial in the long run.

You can begin by investing in startups and private companies. They can prove to be lucrative with time. Also, you are more likely to get a company that is in line with your values if you properly research.

When investing, it is wise to balance your portfolio by investing in public and private companies. Look out for companies that allow you to direct invest in them so you can increase wealth.

Investing in companies

Not every small business is a private company and vice versa. But they share almost the same process of investing. Regardless of size, the company must prove it growth potential to be able to sell shares to the shareholders.

You will need to invest in the company directly. That means rather than buying from stock exchange, you deal directly with the company.

Many private companies and startups possess, more benefits than public companies. You will have a direct relationship with the owners of the companies and you get more say on the workings of the company.

No matter the type of company you choose to invest in, there's a similar process that applies to making your choice.

There are so many companies you can plough your money into despite your level of experience in the market place. This will take time and a deep research. There are many online platforms that provide info on these companies. You can simply look them up and you will see the companies and investment opportunities you can get involved in.

This is where the main difference between public and private companies lay. Public companies are required to give out their financial state to the SEC but the same is not for private companies. So, it can get more difficult to know more about some private companies.

Set up meetings with the business owners

Owners of businesses know that having an investor is crucial to business success. Now you put your money into a company, have a chat with the owners. Create a rapport with them. Get a private company with record of growth and solid business practices. You can go with a bunch of questions to ask them.

Inquire about the business plan. Their business plan will show the company's potential to grow and to adapt to changing conditions like recession and others.

Review their financial statements, and other documents. By talking to them, you can verify any information or doubt you have about them. The questions you ask must be detailed. You need to discuss the following:

1. Their current consuming audience and the basis for their product's success.
2. The change their product brings to the market.
3. The business mistakes they have made and their recovery style.
4. Who supports them and believes in them?

Know more about their modus operandi

The way a business operates is one of the most obvious ways of knowing the growth level and trajectory the business will take. The company you want to invest in must have a business model that records growth, otherwise, there's no need to invest in it.

A great business model shows the following:

1. Debt
2. Budget
3. Equity
4. Acquisition of assets
5. Fund allocation

From the model, you should know the source of the company's money, value of the company and whatever is needed for it to succeed.

Also, the business model will show you how the company makes use of its components successfully. These components are the skills of its employees, the policies of the company, technology and so on

Being informed about the operating model of a company also shows that it can thrive amidst challenges and produce high quality products or services. It will also answer your question on whether your money will be used wisely.

Carry out negotiation on terms of investment

One thing about investing in a private company is that you can negotiate your terms rather than just buy stocks off the public market. Setting your investment terms is beyond deciding on a fitting price. As you negotiate, ask questions regarding the safeguarding methods like:

1. In what ways will my investment be used?
2. Will you be paid dividends or a part of the profit?
3. What ways does the company reach out to its investors?

4. Will I be able to participate on board?
5. Will I vote to contribute to decisions made by the company?
6. If the company is spending more than a defined amount, will my approval be taken?
7. How do I leave the company?

You should know the type of investment you want to make, if it is a debt or equity investment. Both investments are lucrative, yet they are different in terms of purchase and selling. Based on the investment you will buy; your investment strategy will see some adjustments.

A debt instrument offers low risk for little returns. This investment lacks the volatility of markets like stocks. It is also illiquid. Still, it's a consistent way to create wealth although slower.

An equity investment fluctuates often. Though they are known to fare better than stocks, they are liquid with higher risks and greater returns on investment.

Investing in equity means you own a part of the company. Your share value will increase or decrease based on the company's performance. On the other side, you can easily lose money since there is little guarantee you will be paid.

Equity investment's value are determined by external factors like the social issues, political climate, government policies etc.

It is difficult if not impossible to say which investment fares better. Aside their own unique gain rate, each also possess its own risk potential. The one you choose should depend on your financial situation and risk level.

If you have a long-term goal, you can use debt instrument. With it, you will receive steady but lo risks return.

If you want a fast-paced investing and losing money is a small thing to you, you can choose equity investments. You tend to benefit faster from it.

Close your deal

After negotiating your terms with the company to a satisfactory point, you can close your delay. This is where the paperwork comes in. although before you have signed other agreement and confidentiality documents.

As you invest, you are expected to read and approve the following:

1. Stock purchase agreement

2. registration rights agreement

3. term sheet

4. certificate of incorporation

5. Voting agreement

6. legal opinion and many others

This may look too much but these agreements are for your protection and the protection of the company. When you review and sign them, you can discuss with the owners on terms and know what your investment can do for you both.

Investing in a company that is socially responsible

Now investors are ploughing funds into companies that share the same values with them. The word of a company on being socially responsible is enough to rely on. you can make use of robo advisers and investment apps to know the social responsibility level of a company.

A robo advisor

A robo advisor will not only guide you on effective ways to use your money, it can help you build a socially responsible portfolio of compan-ies. You can check out robo advisors like Betterment, Wealth simple, Personal Capital etc.

As you research a company, look out for:

1. The way they value relationships. Do they care about their workers, investors and partners?
2. The commitment factor. How trustworthy is the company? Does it live up to its word?
3. Involvement in social issues. Are they active in socially responsible activities or od they stand aside?
4. Customer relationship. Do they understand their customers problems and provide what they need, or does the company care more about its pockets?

HOW TO INVEST IN PUBLIC COMPANIES?

Beginners' investors often begin with public companies. While this is advantageous, they are not always the better option. Since these company types has to register with SEC, their records can be easily found. Because of its less personal appeal, you are less likely to negotiate before buying.

You can buy public owned shares from the stock market. You can make use of online brokers like Public app, Robinhood to make investment easier and more seamless.

Additionally, you can make use of robo advisors if you want to avoid the cost of human beings. You will also get financial tools to improve your investments.

Still, financial advisors are important. They can give you more useful advice as beginners. The advisor will discuss your investment goals and help you create a portfolio that aligns with those goals. He or she will also offer advice on how much your portfolio should be split among different assets classes.

Ensure you have deeply researched your advisor before hiring. You can make use of paladin registry to start with.

Investing in startups

Startups s no a losing option despite the fact that you may not record a return on investment for the first two years at least. So, before investing in a startup, ensure you have patience and more risk allowance.

Also, do you research on the company and its business plans. Communicate with the owners and question them on their operating models.

There are other ways you can invest in startups. You can make us of Crowdfunding online, buy equity with a small company and take advantage of Pre-IPO opportunities.

Crowdfunding

This is the opportunity for newbie investors to engage in startups. This allows for lesser negotiations since you pool funds alongside others as a group having set some conditions.

This method allows you to invest lesser than you would have if you dealing directly with the company. You can used crowdfunding sites like Start Engine and Seed Invest to begin investing with as low as $100.

Buying equity with a small company

While platforms like Seed Invest allow you to purchase equity via them, you may desire a deeper connection with the company you want to invest in.

These ways can help you in building investments with time, nut the success is dependent on the companies you invest in. at times buying equity directly from the company gives you a push ahead of your competition before other investors get to know about it.

Just as you would research for investments online, you can also search for opportunities to invest locally. While you can also apply crowdfunding, investing locally depends more on networking.

So, by joining a local investment network you can more contact with similar investors around you that can support you in funding startups. While these investors don't necessarily invest groupwise, they will share chances and opportunities and allow investors to make the decision to invest or not. When you join these groups, you would gain more knowledge and learn the methods they use.

The flow of money into the global economy has increased the prices of many assets. Daily real estate prices continue to advance and Bitcoin is at it all time high, recording over $50000 in February. As at February, there were concerns over the increased interest rates which saw the S%P 500 gaining a bit more. Still some companies have even noted to hold the best stocks you can invest in:

1. Bumble

This is still under speculation but the great risk associated with it will tantamount to the great reward it is bound to bring. Bumble is popular in the online dating industry. Currently, its evaluation is worth over $8billion.

2. Walt Disney co.

This is noted as one of the best stocks for this year because it has held an attractive spot for months on end. One of its programs, Disney+, continues to amass a streaming audience of over 90 million subscribers. Future projections show that the company expects over 250 million subscribers in 2024.

3. Goldman Sachs

Bank stocks have a high tendency of benefitting from increasing rates. The Goldman Sachs recorded 23% growth in revenue in the global markets. It current holds a price earnings ratio of 13 which makes it an attractive company to invest in.

4. Viacom CBS

this media giant is gradually making its way back despite the beatings from the Covid pandemic. Its massive growth plans are greatly applauded. This company owns some of the most popular programs, the likes of Nickelodeon, MTV, Showtime among others. It recently launched Paramount+ earlier this month.

5. Alibaba group

This tops the list of best stocks to invest in. this Chinese ecommerce giant has a dip in its shares price last month. That dip allowed investors to buy into the company at a relatively fair price. Currently, it records 20 times its earnings and is expected to have a 30% growth in revenue by 2022.

This company remains the best, high quality stock trading at a price earnings ratio of 23.

CHAPTER 10

THE NEED TO MAKE PLANS AHEAD OF TIME

Many people make financial plans once a significant event happens in their lives. It is now after that occurrence that they realize financial planning should have begun early before. Financial planning is essential to wealth building, financial security and retiring early. there's no better time than now to begin.

To create a financial plan does not require you to be wealthy. In fact, setting up your plan early benefits you in many ways.

1. Since you have a plan, you are more prepared. Every single dollar you earn serves a purpose and will be channeled to a worthwhile activity. Even if an unexpected activity occurs, you are less likely to fall apart.

2. You will not be in a rush. Rather you will feel freer and more confident. Your peace of mind will be gratifying and you will feel more secure.

3. You have created goals which means you have something you're working towards. Also, your goals can be refined with time. Having those goals gives you the freedom to spend without guilt because you have a plan and you abide by it.

4. You also get to know when you have amassed enough to support you during retirement. Knowing you are financially stable will make things less stressful and worrisome for you. You focus your energy on important activities because you have a clearer picture of your financial future.

5. As you plan your finances, you would have established a relationship with a financial advisor. That way, when things get tough, you can easily get your doubts clarified. there's no bad time to plan for your future, neither is there a perfect time as well. you may doesn't need to be full proof. However, having a plan allows you to achieve your goals. It is the ma you use to guide you on your financial journey. The essence of things is to plan. Leaving your financial future to chance is disastrous.

HOW TO AVOID POOR INVESTMENT IDEAS

There are many terrible investment ideas touted by financial gurus and individuals. You can avoid falling into those trips when you know what to look out for and ask questions for clarification. You can avoid making poor investment by following these rules:

Investments with little marketability

Some investments are easy to get into but not out of. Those investments are known as illiquid assets. That means that the asset lacks trading volume. Some of them include private placements, partnerships on real estate, reits that are not publicly traded are anything referred to as an alternative investment.

Having excess money in illiquid investment will give you little access to your funds. Usually, these investments offer high returns only to trap you once you get in. there is also the risk of losing your entire investment. Even if you want to invest, ensure to diversify and put in no more than 10-15% of your money in these opportunity types.

Investments with upfront commissions

These must be completely avoided. They mostly turn out bad because no one, not even your advisor will give you additional service or educate you once you have made the investment. Examples of this include variable universal life insurance, A share funds etc.

Whenever you pay a commission upfront, your financial advisor is not moved to provide services to you. Now, there are different ways you can get financial advice without paying commissions. Even though there are times when you may need to pay a small commission to invest, those times should be minimal.

On big exception is real estate since the realtor is not responsible for servicing for property. So, you are required to pay a commission upfront. The jo of the realtor is simply to find the best property deals for you.

Investments that are confusing

When you don't understand a particular investment, it is better to avoid it. Sometimes, a good investment can become a bad one if you don't understand how it works. If the opportunity interests you but sounds difficult, you can simply ask questions for clarity. Another choice is to walk away. You can also get a professional to help you analyze the investment.

Investments of the same type

While diversifying is a great decision, placing all your money into one investment type is a terrible decision. an asset class can be of value to your portfolio but don't invest all you have into just one. Some of these include;

Reits-while reits are great investment, they should form a small part of your portfolio

Annuities-these can provide good guarantees. However, do not put in all your money into it because of the fees and low liquidity ration.

Tax advantaged accounts

It is essential to build a balance among your tax advantaged accounts. Putting all your money in such accounts will backfire especially when it's time to pay taxes.

As you diversify, you can hire a professional or firm to manage your diverse investments. Some noteworthy firms are;

-mutual fund companies like Fidelity or Vanguard

-brokerage firms like Charles Schwab or TD Ameritrade etc.

BUILDING A NEW LIFE AFTER RETIREMENT

You have finally retired and you look forward to affecting the already made plans you have. You find out that there are some adjustments you need to make. You may discover that the house id too big for you and your spouse or vice versa. You are used to being in the way of your spouse. This is where all those planned activities come into play.

Part of your new activities may be to spend ample time with your spouse, but you will also want to spend some time apart from each other. You will want to send time with friends or continue some activities that you were doing before you retired. Finding out that you need time alone from your spouse sometimes, you can convert certain parts of your home into your personal space. You and your spouse can have separate offices or relaxation dens. you both may not be used to having each other around all the time, but you don't want to leave home in the bid to have some personal tie.

Since the extra income is not available, you both will need to review your budget. Doing so will help you know where you stand financially and to evaluate your spending decisions before financial issues arise. You probably have money but you may not want to spend it so fast. If need be, you can create separate discretionary accounts.

Plan on the times you both will review your finances and the performance of any investment you have. You can make it once or twice a year or quarterly. If one person is doing the bookkeeping, the other should be informed about what's going on. the other is not keeping track of the details of expenses and investment will still need to know everything about their financial status.

Even if one of you should carry out the money tracking, it should never be a burden. Both you and your spouse should come together to understand your financial situation. Both of you must feel in control and have deeper understanding of your money and your growing funds every time.